Life + Soul
LIBRARY

Why are people different colours?

Big issues for little people around identity and diversity

Written by **Dr Emma Waddington** + **Dr Christopher McCurry**

Illustrated by **Louis Thomas**

Frances Lincoln
Children's Books

Contents

How to use this book

This book has been conceived for you to share with a child. Each spread is themed by topic and should be used as a discussion point to help you to talk through common issues in childhood.

STEP 1   Turn to the spread featuring the issue you wish to discuss with a child.

STEP 2   Before sitting down with the child, read the advice from the authors explaining some common causes of behavioural patterns, and some tips on how to tackle them.

STEP 3   Direct the child's attention to the illustration and read the story which accompanies the scenario in front of them. This is a safe and non-confrontational way to approach a topic.

STEP 4   Explore the issue further with the conversational prompts which encourage the child to empathise with the scenario. This should ease you in to having a conversation with them about their own behaviour.

Ibrahim stood in the crowd, looking wide-eyed at all the people around him and asked his dad, "Why are people different colours?"

How will this book help you talk to a child?

Diversity is all around us. From snowflakes to flowers to human beings, there is a seemingly endless variety within basic forms. Our children notice these differences, their curiosity is activated, and the "why?" questions begin. As carers we have an opportunity to shape our children's ideas about themselves and the world down to the architecture of their brains.

Curiosity is an essential ingredient for a child's developing brain, and our response plays a key part in that development. Most questions from children are pretty mundane, but now and again they will ask something that leaves us dumbfounded, surprised, or, at times, upset, meaning that we cannot answer without further thought and time. In this book, we will explain some commonly asked questions from children, offer advice on how to respond (and explain why your answers matter!), and talk about how to manage the emotions that may come with these discussions. If you need further support in certain areas, turn to the back of this book where you will find resources to help you.

How is a child's behaviour connected to their developing brain?

As children explore and learn, they are building their brain – in particular, the front of their brains. This is the part that helps us make sense of our world. In adults, it is huge, and this allows us to override the reactive back of the brain in order to slow down, reason, evaluate and make sense of situations and experiences.

However, up to the age of four, it is the back of a child's brain that dominates. This

> **As children notice differences, their curiosity is activated**

back part of the brain – also known as our reptilian brain – is responsible for letting us know when something bad is happening and informing us that we need to run away. This is a reactive part of the brain that was once essential for survival and is, by nature, very inflexible. This is why it can be so hard to calm a tantrum in full blast.

Unfortunately, the front and back of the brain are poorly connected – especially in the very young. So when the amygdala, the specific part of the reptilian brain responsible for emotions such as fear and anger, fires up, it is very hard to tame.

As carers, we want our children to develop the front of the brain, as this will help them to manage their behaviour. This means that we can reason with them when they are in the midst of a fierce tantrum; we can ask them to wait, and they will, before jumping out into the road, and so on.

So as children ask questions and hear your answers, these experiences are also shaping their brains – in particular, their frontal lobes. As they build these networks, our children will be better able to manage social situations, build stronger bonds and act in ways that bring them joy and happiness.

Why is what you say to a child important?

You are a child's first source of 'truth' in the world, and are responsible for shaping their beliefs, concerns, views, values and principles concerning how to behave... And the values you instil in a child now will probably continue to influence them for the rest of their life. By 'values' we mean what a child will find important and fulfilling in life: the direction they will want to take. We can also see it as their point of reference or a compass that will help them navigate through some of life's choppy waters.

As the world we live in becomes increasingly small, a 'global village', our children will be introduced to a myriad of ethnicities and cultures like no generation before them. As we continue to bring persons with disabilities out of the shadows and into mainstream life, our children will have classmates and coworkers and neighbours who are competent and capable within their differences. We want our children to meet this world with enthusiasm. Perhaps the child you care for is one with some differences.

> We want our children to meet this world of diversity with enthusiasm

What are some basic things to think about when a child asks about diversity?

A child's awareness of differences among people begins with noticing physical attributes. Children as young as age two self-identify as a boy or a girl. With age comes increasing awareness of physical appearance, including basic height and weight differences among people as well as skin and hair colour. Also with age comes awareness of cultural and societal differences and expectations. For example, between age three and four, children start to differentiate between 'boy' toys (e.g., trucks) and 'girl' toys (e.g., dolls). From this point on, curiosity about differences in physical appearance takes off with questions about ethnicity soon to follow at about age five.

Encountering a person, especially another child, with a physical disability can be alarming. In times of upset and uncertainty, your child's question may be less about obtaining factual information (though that can be important) but serve also as an attempt to convey some basic concern or emotion, such as anxiety or confusion. Such questions become an opportunity for carers to convey understanding and acceptance. At these times it's important for carers to check their own emotional responses, to consider their values in terms of acceptance and inclusiveness, and to model compassion, understanding, and celebration for the multitude of differences found in our fellow human beings.

Answers to questions must of course be age-appropriate for the child. And, as a child grows and reaches new developmental phases, he obtains more sophisticated capacities for thinking about (and questioning) the world around him. This means questions can resurface years later as children grow: "That boy in my class two years ago, the one who never talked, did he have autism?" That may then be an opportunity to provide a little more information as appropriate, and to help the child develop a more sophisticated understanding of these issues.

It is important to help children look 'beyond'

> ## A child's awareness of differences begins with noticing physical attributes

the differences and to see what unites us as people. Sometimes we talk about children with 'special needs' when, in fact, people with disabilities have the same needs we all have: for safety, for respect, for friendship, and for laughter. In a similar way, people from different ethnic or religious backgrounds are at their core, 'at heart', people who all want the same basic things for themselves, for their own children, and for their communities.

> It's important to help children look 'beyond' the differences and to see what unites us as people

You may live in a community that is rich in diversity and your child may have ample opportunities to encounter, learn from, and grow from contact with people of different ethnicities and abilities. If there is less diversity where you live, consider bringing films, books, food and music into your child's world that celebrate diversity. The resources at the end of this book will give you some ideas.

Why is good communication so important?

We have an opportunity in these early years to set some good routines and habits that a child will maintain in their adult years. By finding ways to encourage a child's curiosity as they question the world around them, we will be activating their brains in different ways... By giving them reasons that are consistent with what matters to them in that moment, we will be helping them find meaning in their actions.

By helping them feel understood and heard, we will be helping you to manage some of the emotions that arise.

By being consistent in your expectations and setting good routines, you will be communicating the importance in these actions.

Together we will work on making you feel more confident in navigating the torrent of questions that we are faced with daily with commitment and care.

We look forward to working in this new way together!

Ibrahim lived in a small village in the countryside, but this morning he had gone on a trip with his dad to the city.

Everything was so different there! The buildings were really tall, the streets were really wide, and there were so many people.

As he stood in the crowd, Ibrahim looked more closely at all the people around him and asked his dad,

"Why are people different colours?"

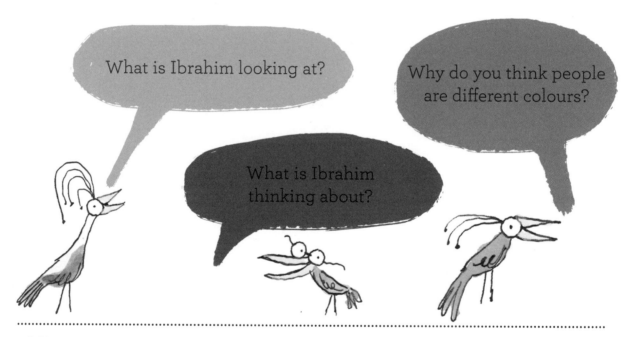

What is Ibrahim looking at?

Why do you think people are different colours?

What is Ibrahim thinking about?

Children are naturally curious. And they are really good at spotting differences. However, deep within the brain, 'difference' can register as 'threat'.

Questions about differences are an important platform for carers to have conversations with children so that differences among people can be understood for what they are: variations on the theme of being human, without seeing them in threatening or judgmental terms.

Young children are often very literal. So respond with a factual answer such as, "Just like some people are quite tall and others are smaller, people can have all sorts of skin colours. But they are just like us."

It is important to maintain composure and not get carried away with what these questions could mean.

However, it is very different if the child is using judgmental words or pointing. In such a case, we want to remind the child of our family values of kindness and respect.

"Why are people different colours?"

Yuki and her brother had been at school. There, the teacher had told Yuki to bring her mum and dad in next week for a parents' evening. Yuki had put her hand up. "I don't have a daddy," she said. "Don't be silly. Everybody has a daddy," said her friend Lola. Yuki thought about this, and when she got home, she asked,

"Why do we not have a daddy?"

Why does Yuki look alarmed?

What makes a family a family?

Do you know children who don't have a daddy?

Children are naturally conservative. They like to be the same as others in many ways, until adolescence, when being unique becomes important.

However, in the early years, children generally don't like to stand out – and the 'norm' is still to have a daddy. However, it is quite common now for single mothers to be raising children for whom there has never been an adult male presence, and these families can flourish. A child in these circumstances can simply be told that not every family must have two parents and there are other important grown-ups who love and cherish you in addition to your mother.

If Daddy is not around due to death or divorce, both of these circumstances may still carry a lot of grief. The question may be calling for love and validation. Respond with love and concern. The child is probably not asking for a factual answer. Simply naming the emotion ('sadness') or the wish that may be behind this question, will likely be sufficient to diffuse it.

"Why do we not have a daddy?"

Abby had invited Olivia round to play. Olivia had brought a new toy with her – a little horse, which she was very proud of. But when she got to Abby's house, she saw that Abby had been given a huge pony for her birthday! Olivia thought Abby's toy looked much better than hers.

On the way home, Olivia said, "Dad, Abby has much bigger toys than me."

"Well, Abby has more in some ways, and you have more in other ways," replied her dad. Abby asked,

"Why do some people have more than others?"

How is Olivia feeling?

What would it be like to have everything you wanted?

What are the things you really like that don't cost money?

Young children are very sensitive to fairness. They will immediately notice if someone is getting more than them in terms of sweets, presents, time with a carer, and so on.

All these differences call for them to state with contempt, "It's not fair."

It's hard for young ones to comprehend having 'less' or 'more' without feeling hard done by or triumphant, both of which are troubling. Take a matter-of-fact approach. Discuss all of the many ways

they have more and less than their friends – more hair, a smaller car, a bigger bed, more puzzles etc. Make it fun to talk about difference, so that difference in itself isn't a problem. It just is a part of life. Validate that you would like more of some things, too (and possibly less of others!).

Connect your child to the things your family values: fun time together over material possessions: being generous and charitable to those less fortunate, gratitude for what we have.

"Why do some people have more than others?"

Angus had gone to visit his grandma. On the corner of her street, a man was sitting on the curb with a plate on the ground in front of him. Angus watched as people passing by stopped to drop some coins onto the man's plate.

"Why are people giving that man money, Grandma?" Angus asked.

"Well, they want to give him their change so that he can buy something to eat. He may not have much food," she answered. Angus replied to her,

"Why do some people have more food than others?"

What is Angus doing?

Is this something that worries you?

Have you ever seen someone that doesn't have enough food?

***

This is a more specific instance of the previous question. The sad reality of childhood these days is that they are exposed to media and news more often and with more intensity than earlier generations.

Some children get very upset to hear about other children in the world who go without basic amenities like food and water. It doesn't seem fair. And it isn't. Children at this age are not ready for long sermons on geopolitics or issues of war and refugees. Instead, invite them to tell you how they feel about it and share any worries they may have. Perhaps they fear that one day it might be them. Validate their fears in the sense that you're acknowledging the presence of those thoughts and feelings, not saying that those ideas are actually true or may become true. Consider sheltering them from watching the news themselves. Instead, tell them what is happening in the world – if it is necessary – in a very factual and reassuring way.

"Why do some people have more food than others?"

A ngus and his friend Abby were playing at his grandma's house. "Your grandma is really wrinkly!" said Abby.

"I can be wrinkly, too," said Angus, pushing together his cheeks.

Abby thought this was really funny! She fell about laughing. After she got up again, she said, "Your wrinkles go away again. But look, your grandma's wrinkles are stuck!"

Later on, Angus was thinking about this, and asked his mum,

"Why does Grandma have wrinkles?"

Have you seen the wrinkles on Grandma or Grandad's face?

What is Angus doing?

Have you noticed any other differences in Grandma?

Children don't miss a thing! Any physical differences they notice can prompt them to ask questions.

Carers answering this query may explain to the child that the skin is connected to our muscles, so it moves as our muscles move, for example, when we smile or frown. And with age, our skin gets less elastic, so it doesn't just bounce back into place. Instead, it leaves a mark, like a crease in your trousers. The older you get, the more laughs and frowns you make, the more creases you have!

The carer might want to remind the child that Grandma may not want to talk or hear about the creases, or wrinkles, in her face. Some people don't like to hear about their differences.

The child may be thinking that wrinkles and other physical aspects of aging are signs of illness and so there may be some anxiety attached to these kinds of questions. You could give some reassurance that wrinkles, greying hair, and the like are natural and not harmful in any way... And certainly not contagious!

"Why does Grandma have wrinkles?"

Ibrahim had been at school. There, his teacher had set them some homework.

"Now, everyone in this class is different, and that is something you should all be proud of – you are all special and unique in your own ways," she had said. "Tonight, try to write down five things that make you, you."

When he got home, Ibrahim went up to look at himself in the mirror, to see if he could find a way that he could be special. When his mum came in, he asked her,

"What makes me, me?"

This is a tough question. It invokes philosophical answers! Or perhaps it just calls for giving the child lots of examples of how they are different to everyone else, especially their siblings.

The carer can help by listing many of the child's attributes: what they like to do, what they like to eat, their strengths.

As the child gets older, this question may ask for more. Children begin to recognise that they are 'different', or at least behave differently, around their friends compared with time spent with parents and so on. Or at times it seems that 'my sad self' and 'my happy self' are two different people: which is the 'real' me? The truth is that they all are the real you experiencing different moods and behaviours in different ways because of the situation you're in.

"What makes me, me?"

Abby was at school when she found out that she was going to have a new teacher for maths called Mrs Kamal.

On the way home, Abby told her mum about her day. "Mrs Kamal is our new teacher," she said.

"Do you like her?" asked Abby's mum.

"Yes, she's very pretty, and she wears earrings that make a jingly sound when she talks, and she had a scarf over her head." Then Abby asked,

"Why does our teacher wear a headscarf?"

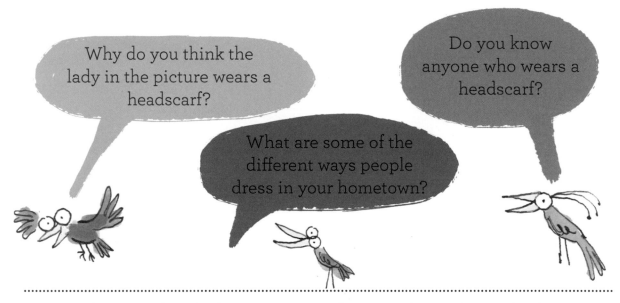

Why do you think the lady in the picture wears a headscarf?

What are some of the different ways people dress in your hometown?

Do you know anyone who wears a headscarf?

In our age of international travel and immigration, this question allows the carer to help the child become open and curious about difference, as opposed to feeling anxious or judgmental.

In our more fluid and open society, children are going to be exposed to lots of differences in the way people dress, think, behave and look. The carer can explain to the child that in the same way a person may have different eye colours, language, and choice in music, they also have different religions. With religion often come traditions in the form of celebrations, what people eat, or how they dress. Some women who practice Islam as their religion choose to wear a headscarf. You can explain that it helps some people feel close to their history, traditions and values. Like so many of these questions we encounter, this asks us as carers to think of our own values and what we want to instil in our children, especially if we want to reinforce the values of respect, acceptance and open-mindedness.

"Why does our teacher wear a headscarf?"

Olivia was having lunch at school with Ibrahim and Mark. They queued up to be given their food by the dinner lady, Mrs Custard.

"Pork chops today!" she said, as she handed Abby her lunch. Next in line was Mark. "And some special turkey legs for you, Mark," she added.

"Why do you have something different to me?" Olivia asked Mark.

"I can't eat pork," said Mark.

Later that evening, Olivia was thinking about this, and she asked her dad,

"Why doesn't Mark eat pork?"

What are Mark's friends thinking?

Do any of your friends eat different foods to you?

What are some of the reasons people may not eat certain foods?

Similar to the previous question, this is a chance for the carer to help their child understand people's traditions, and remain open-minded and respectful of the choices people make.

As before, carers can explain that people choose to practise religion and that each religion carries certain beliefs. Islamic and Jewish traditions have certain beliefs about avoiding pork. Many years ago, Roman Catholics did not eat meat on Fridays as one of their traditions. It is helpful to frame it in terms of choices

and beliefs as this will help children feel open to them and less judgmental.

It is important not to express judgment on the behaviour and instead simply describe it as such – a practice based on their religious beliefs and traditions. What are some important beliefs and traditions in your family? How do these help connect us to our histories, our values, and what we hold to be important?

"Why doesn't Mark eat pork?"

Ibrahim was out shopping with his mum. He was helping her fill the trolley with all the things she needed. "Carrots, please, Ibrahim," she asked, "and leeks, squash and broccoli." He put them all in. "And some pineapple, nectarines and pears, please," she added.

"Mum! When are we going to get some meat?" he asked. "We can't eat just vegetables forever!"

"But whyever not?" asked his mum. "You know, some people don't eat meat at all." Ibrahim couldn't believe it, and asked,

"Why do some people not eat meat?"

Do you know anyone who doesn't eat meat?

In what other ways are people different from each other?

Why doesn't Ibrahim eat meat?

This question is slightly different to the previous ones, as it may or may not be a choice based on religion. Not eating meat could be a religious, ethical, or health-related decision – or one simply based on preference.

If it is something you have chosen to do in your home, then you can reinforce the choices as a carer based on your family values. In this case the question might be, "Why do some people eat meat?" In any case, the carer can reflect on the values you hold as individuals and as a family, and how these values help us decide what to eat and not eat. Others may make other decisions for themselves and their families. Children are fairly pragmatic, so wherever possible, they will be satisfied with a pragmatic answer.

"Why do some people not eat meat?"

Ibrahim was at a birthday party. There were lots of new children at the party that he didn't know, including a girl in a wheelchair. He had never seen someone in a wheelchair before, but she was lots of fun. They tied balloons to the back of her chair and took it in turns to push her round in the garden really fast. Ibrahim wondered why everyone didn't have one!

"You can't have a wheelchair, Ibrahim," said his mum. "Only people who need a wheelchair use one." Ibrahim asked,

"How come she is in a wheelchair?"

What is happening in the picture? Who is having the most fun?

How does the girl in the wheelchair feel? Why?

How would you help someone in a wheelchair?

Older children become more aware of their fragility and are more curious and sensitive of those who appear to be struggling physically and emotionally.

It can be especially hard for them to see other children who are suffering, or worse off than them. It may elicit anxiety about their own vulnerability. As a carer we can explain that most of us are born with everything we need, but some are born with parts that are not working as well – perhaps in this case the legs. Sometimes a person has an injury that requires *them to use a wheelchair or crutches. We can reflect on how they are still similar to us in that they want to have friends, love to play and enjoy movies. This will help children connect with the disability as only one part of them. As a carer, we can also emphasise our value of caring for others by reflecting how sometimes it can be really hard for children with disabilities to do things we do easily, and it takes them a lot of courage, so they would really value having friends who want to help them and have fun together.*

"How come she is in wheelchair?"

A ngus had gone to his friend Lila's house to play. Earlier that day, Lila had been to a place called 'the opticians'. There she had practised her reading and afterwards they had given her a pair of glasses. Angus was quite surprised when he saw her at first, because she looked a bit different.

"Do you want to try them on?" asked Lila. When Angus put them on, suddenly everything looked bigger, a bit like when he looked through his grandpa's binoculars. On the way home, he asked his mum,

"Why does Lila wear glasses?"

What is Angus doing?

Have you tried on anyone's glasses?

Are there things that you need help with?

As carers, we can explain that we are all different – some of us have short hair, others long – some of us like broccoli, others prefer spinach. In the same way, difference extends to our eyesight so that some of us may see better than others. And some of us may need special glasses to help us see as well as we need to.

We can also explain that our eyes are shaped differently – like our noses or legs. Some eyes are too long or too short, or don't bend the light in the right way, which affects how well we see. The glasses help bend the light in such a way that our eyes can't do alone. This helps us to see better.

It is important to remind children that people may be somewhat nervous about needing to wear glasses, especially when they are new and just getting used to them. So, if a classmate or friend has glasses, we should never tease them about it or in any way make them feel bad for needing help to see as well as they can.

"Why does Lila wear glasses?"

It was the school holidays and Angus was at home with his grandma. "Grandma, why can't Mum and Dad stay and play with us, too?" asked Angus.

"I'm sure they would like that very much, Angus, but they are grown-ups and they have to do their jobs," answered Grandma.

"Did you have a job, Grandma?" asked Angus.

"Yes!" answered Grandma. "I was a scientist, just like your daddy." Angus thought about this and asked,

"What will I be when I grow up?"

What is Angus thinking?

Do you have any ideas about growing up that worry you?

What are some of the things you would like to do?

Children learn early on that they will become adults, and adults are special people who do special things, like being a policeman, a doctor, or an astronaut.

At a certain age, adults start asking children what they want to be when they grow up. Initially, it appears as a fairly innocuous question. Yet, as carers, we are consistently shaping our children. A child's surroundings (including their carers, peers, choice of books and teachers) lead them to link their identity to a career. They see that as adults we add value to others depending on their choice of careers. So when this question is posed as carers we want to think about the value we want to instil. What do we want to reinforce as their identity? Do we want them to be open-minded and define themselves as multifaceted (e.g., I will be a person who has children/a farm/a home/a partner/lots of friends, will enjoy music and so on)? We want to nurture the curiosity and excitement that comes from engaging life fully, so that it will carry our children into a bright and valued future.

"What will I be when I grow up?"

Further reading and resources

Books to read with children

Downey, R. *Love is a Family.* (New York: Harper Collins, 2001)

Hammill, E. *Over the Hills and Far Away: A Treasury of Nursery Rhymes from Around the World.* (London: Francis Lincoln Publishers, 2014)

Hoberman, M. A. *All Kinds of Families!* (New York: Little, Brown and Co, 2009)

Thomas, P. *Don't Call Me Special: A First Look at Disability.* (Hauppauge, NY: Barron's Educational Series, 2002)

See also:

theguardian.com/childrens-books-site/2014/oct/13/50-best-culturally-diverse-childrens-books. *The Guardian's 50 best books on cultural diversity*

ccbc.education.wisc.edu/books/detailListBooks.asp?idBookLists=42. The University of Wisconsin School of Education

Websites

kidshealth.org/parent/positive/talk/tolerance.html. From the Nemours Foundation, a parent's guide to teaching tolerance.

scholastic.com/teachers/article/teaching-diversity-place-begin-0. A guide to teaching diversity, at home or in the classroom, for ages four to eight.

Why are people different colours copyright © Frances Lincoln Ltd 2016
Text copyright © Dr Emma Waddington and Dr Christopher McCurry 2016
Illustrations copyright © Louis Thomas 2016

First published in the UK in 2016 by Frances Lincoln Children's Books,
74–77 White Lion Street, London N1 9PF, UK
QuartoKnows.com
Visit our blogs at QuartoKnows.com

A catalogue record for this book is available from the British Library.

ISBN 978-1-84780-810-3

Edited by Jenny Broom
Designed by Andrew Watson
Production by Laura Grandi
Published by Rachel Williams

Printed in China
1 3 5 7 9 8 6 4 2

MIX
Paper from
responsible sources
FSC® C104723
www.fsc.org